W9-CAL-994

Presented To:

_____

Given By:

_____

On the Date Of:

_____

For I assure you: If you have faith the size of
a mustard seed, you will tell this mountain,
"Move from here to there," and it will move.
Nothing will be impossible for you.

—

Matthew 17:20 HCSB

PROMISES
and
Prayers

for a woman's heart

The quoted ideas expressed in this book (but not Scripture verses) are not, in all cases, exact quotations, as some have been edited for clarity and brevity. In all cases, the author has attempted to maintain the speaker's original intent. In some cases, quoted material for this book was obtained from secondary sources, primarily print media. While every effort was made to ensure the accuracy of these sources, the accuracy cannot be guaranteed. For additions, deletions, corrections, or clarifications in future editions of this text, please write Freeman-Smith.

The Holy Bible, King James Version

The Holy Bible, New King James Version (NKJV) Copyright © 1982 by Thomas Nelson, Inc. Used by permission.

New century Version®. (NCV) Copyright © 1987, 1988, 1991 by Word Publishing, a division of Thomas Nelson, Inc. All rights reserved. Used by permission.

The Holman Christian Standard Bible™ (HCSB) Copyright © 1999, 2000, 2001 by Holman Bible Publishers. Used by permission.

The Holy Bible, New International Version®. (NIV) Copyright © 1973, 1978, 1984 International Bible Society. Used by permission of Zondervan. All rights reserved.

The Holy Bible. New Living Translation (NLT) copyright © 1996 Tyndale Charitable Trust. Used by permission of Tyndale House Publishers.

The New American Standard Bible®, (NASB) Copyright © 1960, 1962, 1963, 1968, 1971, 1972, 1973, 1975, 1977, 1995 by The Lockman Foundation. Used by permission.

Scripture taken from The Message. (MSG) Copyright © 1993, 1994, 1995, 1996, 2000, 2001, 2002. Used by permission of NavPress Publishing Group.

Cover Design by Kim Russell / Wahoo Designs
Page Layout by Bart Dawson

ISBN 978-1-60587-430-2

Printed in the United States of America

1 2 3 4 5—CHG—16 15 14 13 12

PROMISES
and
Prayers

for a woman's heart

TABLE OF CONTENTS

INTRODUCTION

God has given you a book of promises upon which you, as a Christian woman, can and must depend. That book, of course, is the Holy Bible. The Bible is a priceless gift, a tool that God intends for you to use in every aspect of your life. Yet sometimes, you may be tempted to treat the Bible less like a guidebook and more like a history book—don't make that mistake! Instead, trust God's promises and use His Word as an indispensable guide for life here on earth and for life eternal.

This book is a collection of 30 devotional readings chock-full of promises and prayers for your journey. So during the next month, please try this experiment: read a chapter each day. If you're already committed to a daily time of worship, this book will enrich that experience. If you are not, the simple act of giving God a few minutes each morning will change the direction and the quality of your life.

Every day provides opportunities to put God where He belongs: at the center of your life. When you do so, you will worship Him, not just with words, but with deeds. And as you learn to trust the Creator completely and to obey Him faithfully, you'll soon discover that God always keeps His promises. Always!

THE POWER OF HIS PROMISES

Heaven and earth will pass away,
but My words will never pass away.

—

Matthew 24:35 HCSB

Job understood that the ultimate wisdom belongs to God—and nothing has changed since then. God's wisdom is perfect and complete, unfathomable to mere mortals. We can gain limited understanding by studying God's Word, but we can never gain a complete understanding of God's plans, at least not in this lifetime. Still, even when we cannot fathom God's intentions, we can still choose to trust His wisdom.

Where will you place your trust today? Will you depend upon your limited understanding, or will you place your faith in God's perfect wisdom? When you decide whom to trust, you will learn how best to respond to the challenges of everyday life.

Are you tired? Discouraged? Fearful? Be comforted and trust God. Are you worried or anxious? Be confident in God's power and keep studying His Holy Word. Are you confused? Listen to the quiet voice of your Heavenly Father. He is not a God of confusion. Talk with Him; listen to Him; trust Him. He is steadfast, He is always with you, and He is your Protector . . . forever.

Wisdom from God's Holy Word

But the word of the Lord endures forever. And this is the word that was preached as the gospel to you.

1 Peter 1:25 HCSB

All Scripture is inspired by God and is profitable for teaching, for rebuking, for correcting, for training in righteousness, so that the man of God may be complete, equipped for every good work.

2 Timothy 3:16-17 HCSB

For the word of God is living and effective and sharper than any two-edged sword, penetrating as far as to divide soul, spirit, joints, and marrow; it is a judge of the ideas and thoughts of the heart.

Hebrews 4:12 HCSB

The one who is from God listens to God's words. This is why you don't listen, because you are not from God.

John 8:47 HCSB

More Great Ideas

Words fail to express my love for this holy Book, my gratitude for its author, for His love and goodness. How shall I thank him for it?

Lottie Moon

Weave the unveiling fabric of God's word through your heart and mind. It will hold strong, even if the rest of life unravels.

Gigi Graham Tchividjian

The Bible became a living book and a guide for my life.

Vonette Bright

I need the spiritual revival that comes from spending quiet time alone with Jesus in prayer and in thoughtful meditation on His Word.

Anne Graham Lotz

God's Word is a light not only to our path but also to our thinking. Place it in your heart today, and you will never walk in darkness.

Joni Eareckson Tada

The most important thing about the Bible is that it points us to the living Word of God, which is Jesus Christ.

—

Billy Graham

Today's Timely Tip

Charles Swindoll writes, "There are four words I wish we would never forget, and they are, 'God keeps his word.'" And, when it comes to studying God's Word, school is always in session.

Today's Prayer

Dear Lord, Your Scripture is a light unto the world; let me study it, trust it, and share it with all who cross my path. In all that I do, help me be a woman who is a worthy witness for You as I share the Good News of Your perfect Son and Your perfect Word. Amen

DAY 2

PEACE FOR THE JOURNEY

Peace I leave with you, My peace I give to you;
not as the world gives do I give to you.
Let not your heart be troubled,
neither let it be afraid.

—

John 14:27 NKJV

The beautiful words of John 14:27 give us hope: "Peace I leave with you, my peace I give unto you . . . ." Jesus offers us peace, not as the world gives, but as He alone gives. We, as believers, can accept His peace or ignore it.

When we accept the peace of Jesus Christ into our hearts, our lives are transformed. And then, because we possess the gift of peace, we can share that gift with fellow Christians, family members, friends, and associates. If, on the other hand, we choose to ignore the gift of peace—for whatever reason—we cannot share what we do not possess.

As every woman knows, peace can be a scarce commodity in our demanding world. How, then, can we find the peace that we so desperately desire? By turning our days and our lives over to God. Elisabeth Elliot writes, "If my life is surrendered to God, all is well. Let me not grab it back, as though it were in peril in His hand but would be safer in mine!" May we give our lives, our hopes, and our prayers to the Lord, and, by doing so, accept His will and His peace.

Wisdom from God's Holy Word

God has called us to peace.

1 Corinthians 7:15 NKJV

Be of good comfort, be of one mind, live in peace; and the God of love and peace will be with you.

2 Corinthians 13:11 NKJV

For He is our peace.

Ephesians 2:14 HCSB

The result of righteousness will be peace; the effect of righteousness will be quiet confidence forever.

Isaiah 32:17 HCSB

Now the fruit of righteousness is sown in peace by those who make peace.

James 3:18 NKJV

More Great Ideas

When we do what is right, we have contentment, peace, and happiness.

Beverly LaHaye

To know God as He really is—in His essential nature and character—is to arrive at a citadel of peace that circumstances may storm, but can never capture.

Catherine Marshall

I believe that in every time and place it is within our power to acquiesce in the will of God—and what peace it brings to do so!

Elisabeth Elliot

The fruit of our placing all things in God's hands is the presence of His abiding peace in our hearts.

Hannah Whitall Smith

Prayer guards hearts and minds and causes God to bring peace out of chaos.

Beth Moore

Rejoicing is a matter of
obedience to God—
an obedience that will start
you on the road to peace
and contentment.

—

Kay Arthur

Today's Timely Tip

Peace starts at home. You have a big role to play in helping to maintain a peaceful home. It's a big job, so don't be afraid to ask for help . . . especially God's help.

Today's Prayer

Dear Lord, I will open my heart to You. And I thank You, God, for Your love, for Your peace, and for Your Son. Amen

DAY 3

A JOYFUL SPIRIT

These things I have spoken to you,
that My joy may remain in you,
and that your joy may be full.

—

John 15:11 NKJV

God's Word makes it clear: He intends that His joy should become our joy. The Lord intends that believers should share His love with His joy in their hearts. Yet sometimes, amid the inevitable hustle and bustle of life here on earth, we can forfeit—albeit temporarily—God's joy as we wrestle with the challenges of daily living.

Joni Eareckson Tada spoke for Christian women of every generation when she observed, "I wanted the deepest part of me to vibrate with that ancient yet familiar longing, that desire for something that would fill and overflow my soul."

Psalm 100 reminds us that, as believers, we have every reason to celebrate: "Shout for joy to the LORD, all the earth. Worship the LORD with gladness" (vv. 1-2 NIV). These words most certainly apply to you.

Are you a woman whose joy is clearly evident to your family and friends? If so, congratulations—you're doing God's will. But, if you find yourself feeling discouraged or worse, it's time to slow down and have a quiet conversation with your Creator.

If your heart is heavy, turn to Christ. He will give you peace and joy. And if you already have the joy of Christ in your heart, share it freely, just as Christ has freely shared His joy with you.

Wisdom from God's Holy Word

Weeping may spend the night, but there is joy in the morning.

Psalm 30:5 HCSB

Rejoice in the Lord always. I will say it again: Rejoice!

Philippians 4:4 HCSB

Now I am coming to You, and I speak these things in the world so that they may have My joy completed in them.

John 17:13 HCSB

A joyful heart makes a face cheerful.

Proverbs 15:13 HCSB

25

More Great Ideas

If you're a thinking Christian, you will be a joyful Christian.

Marie T. Freeman

There may be no trumpet sound or loud applause when we make a right decision, just a calm sense of resolution and peace.

Gloria Gaither

The Christian lifestyle is not one of legalistic do's and don'ts, but one that is positive, attractive, and joyful.

Vonette Bright

What is your focus today? Joy comes when it is Jesus first, others second . . . then you.

Kay Arthur

Jesus did not promise to change the circumstances around us. He promised great peace and pure joy to those who would learn to believe that God actually controls all things.

Corrie ten Boom

Where the soul is full of
peace and joy,
outward surroundings
and circumstances are of
comparatively little account.

—

Hannah Whitall Smiith

Today's Timely Tip

Joy is contagious. If you have children, remember that a joyful family starts with joyful parents.

Today's Prayer

Dear Lord, You have given me so many blessings, starting with my family. I will keep joy in my heart as I thank You, Lord, for every single blessing You've given me. Amen

EMBRACED BY GOD

For God so loved the world, that he gave his only begotten Son, that whosoever believeth in him should not perish, but have everlasting life.

—

John 3:16 KJV

God's love for you is bigger and better than you can imagine. In fact, God's love is far too big to comprehend (in this lifetime). But this much we know: God loves you so much that He sent His Son Jesus to come to this earth and to die for you. And, when you accepted Jesus into your heart, God gave you a gift that is more precious than gold: the gift of eternal life.

The words of Romans 8 make this promise: "For I am persuaded that neither death nor life, nor angels nor principalities nor powers, nor things present nor things to come, nor height nor depth, nor any other created thing, shall be able to separate us from the love of God which is in Christ Jesus our Lord" (vv. 38-39 NKJV).

Sometimes, in the crush of your daily duties, God may seem far away, but He is not. God is everywhere you have ever been and everywhere you will ever go. He is with you night and day; He knows your thoughts and He hears your prayers. When you earnestly seek Him, you will find Him because He is here, waiting for you to reach out to Him.

Reach out to God today and always. Encourage your family members to do likewise. And then, arm-in-arm with your loved ones, praise God for blessings that are simply too numerous to count.

Wisdom from God's Holy Word

For the Lord is good, and His love is eternal; His faithfulness endures through all generations.

Psalm 100:5 HCSB

[Because of] the Lord's faithful love we do not perish, for His mercies never end. They are new every morning; great is Your faithfulness!

Lamentations 3:22-23 HCSB

Help me, Lord my God; save me according to Your faithful love.

Psalm 109:26 HCSB

Whoever is wise will observe these things, and they will understand the lovingkindness of the Lord.

Psalm 107:43 NKJV

More Great Ideas

Being loved by Him whose opinion matters most gives us the security to risk loving, too— even loving ourselves.

Gloria Gaither

Snuggle in God's arms. When you are hurting, when you feel lonely or left out, let Him cradle you, comfort you, reassure you of His all-sufficient power and love.

Kay Arthur

Jesus loves us with fidelity, purity, constancy, and passion, no matter how imperfect we are.

Stormie Omartian

There is no pit so deep that God's love is not deeper still.

Corrie ten Boom

God is a God of unconditional, unremitting love, a love that corrects and chastens but never ceases.

Kay Arthur

A bird does not know it can fly
before it uses its wings.
We learn God's love in
our hearts as soon as
we act upon it.

—

Corrie ten Boom

Today's Timely Tip

Remember: God's love for you is too big to understand with your brain . . . but it's not too big to feel with your heart.

Today's Prayer

Lord, I know that You love me. I will accept Your love—and share it—today and every day. Amen

YOUR JOURNEY WITH GOD

*For it is God who is working among you both
the willing and the working for His good purpose.*

—

Philippians 2:13 HCSB

"What on earth does God intend for me to do with my life?" It's an easy question to ask but, for many of us, a difficult question to answer. Why? Because God's purposes aren't always clear to us. Sometimes we wander aimlessly in a wilderness of our own making. And sometimes, we struggle mightily against God in an unsuccessful attempt to find success and happiness through our own means, not His.

If you're sincerely seeking God's guidance, He will give it. But, He will make His revelations known to you in a way and in a time of His choosing, not yours, so be patient. If you prayerfully petition God and work diligently to discern His intentions, He will lead you to a place of joyful abundance and eternal peace.

Sometimes, God's intentions will be clear to you; other times, God's plan will seem uncertain at best. But even on those difficult days when you are unsure which way to turn, you must never lose sight of these overriding facts: God created you for a reason; He has important work for you to do; and He's waiting patiently for you to do it.

Wisdom from God's Holy Word

We know that all things work together for the good of those who love God: those who are called according to His purpose.

Romans 8:28 HCSB

I will instruct you and show you the way to go; with My eye on you, I will give counsel.

Psalm 32:8 HCSB

You reveal the path of life to me; in Your presence is abundant joy; in Your right hand are eternal pleasures.

Psalm 16:11 HCSB

Commit your activities to the Lord and your plans will be achieved.

Proverbs 16:3 HCSB

To everything there is a season, a time for every purpose under heaven.

Ecclesiastes 3:1 NKJV

More Great Ideas

Only God's chosen task for you will ultimately satisfy. Do not wait until it is too late to realize the privilege of serving Him in His chosen position for you.

Beth Moore

In the very place where God has put us, whatever its limitations, whatever kind of work it may be, we may indeed serve the Lord Christ.

Elisabeth Elliot

Yesterday is just experience but tomorrow is glistening with purpose—and today is the channel leading from one to the other.

Barbara Johnson

God specializes in things fresh and firsthand. His plans for you this year may outshine those of the past. He's prepared to fill your days with reasons to give Him praise.

Joni Eareckson Tada

Victory is the result of Christ's
life lived out in the believer.
It is important to see that
victory, not defeat,
is God's purpose for
His children.

—

Corrie ten Boom

Today's Timely Tip

God has a wonderful plan for your life. And the time to start looking for that plan—and living it—is now. (Psalm 16:11)

_____

Today's Prayer

Lord, You've got something You want me to do—help me to figure out exactly what it is. Give me Your blessings and lead me along a path that is pleasing to You . . . today, tomorrow, and forever. Amen

DAY 6

OPTIMISM NOW

*Finally brothers, whatever is true, whatever is
honorable, whatever is just, whatever is pure,
whatever is lovely, whatever is commendable—
if there is any moral excellence
and if there is any praise—dwell on these things.*

—

Philippians 4:8 HCSB

Pessimism and Christianity don't mix. Why? Because Christians have every reason to be optimistic about life here on earth and life eternal. Mrs. Charles E. Cowman advised, "Never yield to gloomy anticipation. Place your hope and confidence in God. He has no record of failure."

Sometimes, despite our trust in God, we may fall into the spiritual traps of worry, frustration, anxiety, or sheer exhaustion, and our hearts become heavy. What's needed is plenty of rest, a large dose of perspective, and God's healing touch, but not necessarily in that order.

Today, make this promise to yourself and keep it: vow to be a hope-filled Christian. Think optimistically about your life, your profession, and your future. Trust your hopes, not your fears. Take time to celebrate God's glorious creation. And then, when you've filled your heart with hope and gladness, share your optimism with others. They'll be better for it, and so will you.

Wisdom from God's Holy Word

Make me hear joy and gladness.

Psalm 51:8 NKJV

My cup runs over. Surely goodness and mercy shall follow me all the days of my life; and I will dwell in the house of the Lord Forever.

Psalm 23:5-6 NKJV

But if we hope for what we do not see, we eagerly wait for it with patience.

Romans 8:25 HCSB

For God has not given us a spirit of fearfulness, but one of power, love, and sound judgment.

2 Timothy 1:7 HCSB

Be strong and courageous, all you who put your hope in the LORD.

Psalm 31:24 HCSB

More Great Ideas

The Christian lifestyle is not one of legalistic do's and don'ts, but one that is positive, attractive, and joyful.

Vonette Bright

We may run, walk, stumble, drive, or fly, but let us never lose sight of the reason for the journey, or miss a chance to see a rainbow on the way.

Gloria Gaither

If you can't tell whether your glass is half-empty or half-full, you don't need another glass; what you need is better eyesight . . . and a more thankful heart.

Marie T. Freeman

Don't miss the beautiful colors of the rainbow while you're looking for the pot of gold at the end of it!

Barbara Johnson

The things we think are
the things that feed our souls.
If we think on pure and lovely
things, we shall grow pure and
lovely like them; and
the converse is equally true.

—

Hannah Whitall Smith

Today's Timely Tip

Be positive: If your thoughts tend toward the negative end of the spectrum, redirect them. How? You can start by counting your blessings and by thanking your Father in heaven. And while you're at it, train yourself to begin thinking thoughts that are more rational, more accepting, and more upbeat.

Today's Prayer

Dear Lord, I will look for the best in other people, I will expect the best from You, and I will try my best to do my best—today and every day. Amen

THE GREATEST OF THESE...

Now these three remain: faith, hope, and love.
But the greatest of these is love.

—

1 Corinthians 13:13 HCSB

As a woman, you know the profound love that you hold in your heart for your own family and friends. As a child of God, you can only imagine the infinite love that your Creator holds for you.

God made you in His own image and gave you salvation through the person of His Son Jesus Christ. And now, precisely because you are a wondrous creation treasured by God, a question presents itself: What will you do in response to the Creator's love? Will you ignore it or embrace it? Will you return it or neglect it? That decision, of course, is yours and yours alone.

When you embrace God's love, your life's purpose is forever changed. When you embrace God's love, you feel differently about yourself, your neighbors, your family, and your world. More importantly, you share God's message—and His love—with others.

Your Heavenly Father—a God of infinite love and mercy—is waiting to embrace you with open arms. Accept His love today and forever.

Wisdom from God's Holy Word

I pray that you, being rooted and firmly established in love, may be able to comprehend with all the saints what is the breadth and width, height and depth, and to know the Messiah's love that surpasses knowledge, so you may be filled with all the fullness of God.

Ephesians 3:17-19 HCSB

If I speak the languages of men and of angels, but do not have love, I am a sounding gong or a clanging cymbal.

1 Corinthians 13:1 HCSB

Dear friends, if God loved us in this way, we also must love one another.

1 John 4:11 HCSB

We love because He first loved us.

1 John 4:19 HCSB

Above all, keep your love for one another at full strength, since love covers a multitude of sins.

1 Peter 4:8 HCSB

More Great Ideas

Love is not soft as water is; it is solid as a rock on which the waves of hatred beat in vain.

Corrie ten Boom

Love always means sacrifice.

Elisabeth Elliot

Line by line, moment by moment, special times are etched into our memories in the permanent ink of everlasting love in our relationships.

Gloria Gaither

Love is extravagant in the price it is willing to pay, the time it is willing to give, the hardships it is willing to endure, and the strength it is willing to spend. Love never thinks in terms of "how little," but always in terms of "how much." Love gives, love knows, and love lasts.

Joni Eareckson Tada

It is when we come to
the Lord in our nothingness,
our powerlessness and
our helplessness that He then
enables us to love in a way
which, without Him, would be
absolutely impossible.

—

Elisabeth Elliot

Today's Timely Tip

The key to successful Christian living lies in your submission to the Spirit of God. If you're a Christian, God has commanded you to love people . . . and it's a commandment that covers both saints and sinners.

Today's Prayer

Dear God, let me share Your love with the world. Make me a woman of compassion. Help me to recognize the needs of others. Let me forgive those who have hurt me, just as You have forgiven me. And let the love of Your Son shine in me and through me today, tomorrow, and throughout all eternity. Amen

DAY 8

SENSING GOD'S PRESENCE

Draw near to God,
and He will draw near to you.

—

James 4:8 HCSB

Since God is everywhere, we are free to sense His presence whenever we take the time to quiet our souls and turn our prayers to Him. But sometimes, amid the incessant demands of everyday life, we turn our thoughts far from God; when we do, we suffer.

Do you set aside quiet moments each day to offer praise to your Creator? As a woman who has received the gift of God's grace, you most certainly should. Silence is a gift that you give to yourself and to God. During these moments of stillness, you will often sense the infinite love and power of your Creator—and He, in turn, will speak directly to your heart.

The familiar words of Psalm 46:10 remind us to "Be still, and know that I am God." When we do so, we encounter the awesome presence of our loving Heavenly Father, and we are comforted in the knowledge that God is not just near. He is here.

Wisdom from God's Holy Word

You will seek Me and find Me when you search for Me with all your heart.

Jeremiah 29:13 HCSB

The Lord is near all who call out to Him, all who call out to Him with integrity. He fulfills the desires of those who fear Him; He hears their cry for help and saves them.

Psalm 145:18-19 HCSB

Surely goodness and mercy shall follow me all the days of my life: and I will dwell in the house of the Lord for ever.

Psalm 23:6 KJV

I am not alone, because the Father is with Me.

John 16:32 HCSB

I have set the Lord always before me; because He is at my right hand I shall not be moved.

Psalm 16:8 NKJV

More Great Ideas

If you want to hear God's voice clearly and you are uncertain, then remain in His presence until He changes that uncertainty. Often, much can happen during this waiting for the Lord. Sometimes, he changes pride into humility, doubt into faith and peace.

Corrie ten Boom

Give yourself a gift today: be present with yourself. God is. Enjoy your own personality. God does.

Barbara Johnson

Through the death and broken body of Jesus Christ on the Cross, you and I have been given access to the presence of God when we approach Him by faith in prayer.

Anne Graham Lotz

If your heart has grown cold, it is because you have moved away from the fire of His presence.

Beth Moore

It's a crazy world and life speeds by at a blur, yet God is right in the middle of the craziness. And anywhere, at anytime, we may turn to Him, hear His voice, feel His hand, and catch the fragrance of heaven.

—

Joni Eareckson Tada

Today's Timely Tip

If you're here, God is here. If you're there, God is, too. You can't get away from Him or His love . . . thank goodness!

Today's Prayer

Dear Lord, You are always with me. Thank You for never leaving my side, even for a moment! Amen

DAY 9

FORGIVENESS NOW

And whenever you stand praying, if you have
anything against anyone, forgive him,
so that your Father in heaven may also
forgive you your wrongdoing.

—

Mark 11:25 HCSB

Even the most mild-mannered women will, on occasion, have reason to become angry with the inevitable shortcomings of family members and friends. But wise women are quick to forgive others, just as God has forgiven them.

The commandment to forgive others is clearly a part of God's Word, but oh how difficult a commandment it can be to follow. Because we are imperfect beings, we are quick to anger, quick to blame, slow to forgive, and even slower to forget. No matter. Even when forgiveness is difficult, God's instructions are straightforward: As Christians who have received the gift of forgiveness, we must now share that gift with others.

If, in your heart, you hold bitterness against even a single person, forgive. If there exists even one person, alive or dead, whom you have not forgiven, follow God's commandment and His will for your life: forgive. If you are embittered against yourself for some past mistake or shortcoming, forgive. Then, to the best of your abilities, forget, and move on. Bitterness and regret are not part of God's plan for your life. Forgiveness is. And once you've forgiven others, you can then turn your thoughts to a far more pleasant subject: the incredibly bright future that God has promised.

Wisdom from God's Holy Word

Be merciful, just as your Father also is merciful.

Luke 6:36 HCSB

All bitterness, anger and wrath, insult and slander must be removed from you, along with all wickedness. And be kind and compassionate to one another, forgiving one another, just as God also forgave you in Christ.

Ephesians 4:31-32 HCSB

Then Peter came to Him and said, "Lord, how many times could my brother sin against me and I forgive him? As many as seven times?" "I tell you, not as many as seven," Jesus said to him, "but 70 times seven."

Matthew 18:21-22 HCSB

More Great Ideas

Forgiveness is actually the best revenge because it not only sets us free from the person we forgive, but it frees us to move into all that God has in store for us.

Stormie Omartian

To be a Christian means to forgive the inexcusable, because God has forgiven the inexcusable in you.

C. S. Lewis

God expects us to forgive others as He has forgiven us; we are to follow His example by having a forgiving heart.

Vonette Bright

Forgiveness is the key that unlocks the door of resentment and the handcuffs of hate. It is a power that breaks the chains of bitterness and the shackles of selfishness.

Corrie ten Boom

When God tells us to love
our enemies, he gives,
along with the command,
the love itself.

—

Corrie ten Boom

Today's Timely Tip

Face facts: forgiveness can be a very hard thing to do. No matter. God instructs us to forgive others (and to keep forgiving them), period.

Today's Prayer

Dear Lord, let forgiveness rule my heart, even when forgiveness is difficult. Let me be Your obedient servant, Lord, and let me be a woman who forgives others just as You have forgiven me. Amen

DAY 10

TRUST HIM

Trust in the Lord with all your heart,
and do not rely on your own understanding;
think about Him in all your ways,
and He will guide you on the right paths.

—

Proverbs 3:5-6 HCSB

When our dreams come true and our plans prove successful, we find it easy to thank our Creator and easy to trust His divine providence. But in times of sorrow or hardship, we may find ourselves questioning God's plans for our lives.

On occasion, you will confront circumstances that trouble you to the very core of your soul. It is during these difficult days that you must find the wisdom and the courage to trust your Heavenly Father despite your circumstances.

Are you a woman who seeks God's blessings for yourself and your family? Then trust Him. Trust Him with your relationships. Trust Him with your priorities. Follow His commandments and pray for His guidance. Trust Your Heavenly Father day by day, moment by moment—in good times and in trying times. Then, wait patiently for God's revelations . . . and prepare yourself for the abundance and peace that will most certainly be yours when you do.

Wisdom from God's Holy Word

For the eyes of the Lord range throughout the earth to show Himself strong for those whose hearts are completely His.

2 Chronicles 16:9 HCSB

He granted their request because they trusted in Him.

1 Chronicles 5:20 HCSB

Let us hold fast the confession of our hope without wavering, for He who promised is faithful.

Hebrews 10:23 NKJV

The one who understands a matter finds success, and the one who trusts in the Lord will be happy.

Proverbs 16:20 HCSB

I know whom I have believed and am persuaded that He is able to guard what has been entrusted to me until that day.

2 Timothy 1:12 HCSB

More Great Ideas

Sometimes the very essence of faith is trusting God in the midst of things He knows good and well we cannot comprehend.

Beth Moore

Are you serious about wanting God's guidance to become the person he wants you to be? The first step is to tell God that you know you can't manage your own life; that you need his help.

Catherine Marshall

Do not be afraid, then, that if you trust, or tell others to trust, the matter will end there. Trust is only the beginning and the continual foundation. When we trust Him, the Lord works, and His work is the important part of the whole matter.

Hannah Whitall Smith

Never be afraid to trust an unknown future to a known God.

Corrie ten Boom

We must lay our questions,
frustrations, anxieties,
and impotence at the feet of
God and wait for His answer.
And then receiving it,
we must live by faith.

—

Kay Arthur

Today's Timely Tip

One of the most important lessons that you can ever learn is to trust God for everything, and that includes timing. In other words, you should trust God to decide the best time for things to happen. Sometimes it's hard to trust God, but it's always the right thing to do.

Today's Prayer

Dear Lord, as I take the next steps on my life's journey, let me take them with You. Whatever the coming day may bring, I will thank You for the opportunity to live abundantly. I will be Your faithful, faith-filled servant, Lord—and I will trust You—this day and forever. Amen

THE POWER OF PATIENCE

Rejoice in hope; be patient in affliction;
be persistent in prayer.

—

Romans 12:12 HCSB

Psalm 37:7 commands us to wait patiently for God. But as busy women in a fast-paced world, many of us find that waiting quietly for God is difficult. Why? Because we are fallible human beings seeking to live according to our own timetables, not God's. In our better moments, we realize that patience is not only a virtue, but it is also a commandment from God.

We human beings are impatient by nature. We know what we want, and we know exactly when we want it: NOW! But, God knows better. He has created a world that unfolds according to His plans, not our own. As believers, we must trust His wisdom and His goodness.

God instructs us to be patient in all things. We must be patient with our families, our friends, and our associates. We must also be patient with our Creator as He unfolds His plan for our lives. And that's as it should be. After all, think how patient God has been with us.

Wisdom from God's Holy Word

Love is patient; love is kind.

1 Corinthians 13:4 HCSB

A patient spirit is better than a proud spirit.

Ecclesiastes 7:8 HCSB

Therefore the Lord is waiting to show you mercy, and is rising up to show you compassion, for the Lord is a just God. Happy are all who wait patiently for Him.

Isaiah 30:18 HCSB

Be gentle to everyone, able to teach, and patient.

2 Timothy 2:23 HCSB

My brethren, count it all joy when you fall into various trials, knowing that the testing of your faith produces patience. But let patience have its perfect work, that you may be perfect and complete, lacking nothing.

James 1:2-4 NKJV

More Great Ideas

We must learn to wait. There is grace supplied to the one who waits.

Mrs. Charles E. Cowman

How do you wait upon the Lord? First you must learn to sit at His feet and take time to listen to His words.

Kay Arthur

Waiting is the hardest kind of work, but God knows best, and we may joyfully leave all in His hands.

Lottie Moon

Let me encourage you to continue to wait with faith. God may not perform a miracle, but He is trustworthy to touch you and make you whole where there used to be a hole.

Lisa Whelchel

Waiting is an essential part of spiritual discipline. It can be the ultimate test of faith.

Anne Graham Lotz

You're in a hurry.
God is not.
Trust God.

—

Marie T. Freeman

Today's Timely Tip

Avoid angry outbursts: Sweet words usually work better than sour ones. If you think you're about to say or do something you'll regret later, slow down and take a deep breath, or two deep breaths, or ten, or . . . well you get the idea.

Today's Prayer

Lord, give me patience. When I am hurried, give me peace. When I am frustrated, give me perspective. When I am angry, let me turn my heart to You. Today, let me become a more patient woman, dear Lord, as I trust in You and in Your master plan for my life. Amen

DAY 12

FAITH
IN THE FATHER

*For whatever is born of God overcomes
the world. And this is the victory that has
overcome the world—our faith.*

—

1 John 5:4 NKJV

Asuffering woman sought healing in an unusual way: she simply touched the hem of Jesus' garment. When she did, Jesus turned and said, "Daughter, be of good comfort; thy faith hath made thee whole" (Matthew 9:22 KJV). We, too, can be made whole when we place our faith completely and unwaveringly in the person of Jesus Christ.

Concentration camp survivor Corrie ten Boom relied on faith during ten months of imprisonment and torture. Later, despite the fact that four of her family members had died in Nazi death camps, Corrie's faith was unshaken. She wrote, "There is no pit so deep that God's love is not deeper still." Christians take note: Genuine faith in God means faith in all circumstances, happy or sad, joyful or tragic.

When you place your faith, your trust, indeed your life in the hands of Christ Jesus, you'll be amazed at the marvelous things He can do with you and through you. So strengthen your faith through praise, through worship, through Bible study, and through prayer. Then, trust God's plans. Your Heavenly

Father is standing at the door of your heart. If you reach out to Him in faith, He will give you peace and heal your broken spirit. Be content to touch even the smallest fragment of the Master's garment, and He will make you whole.

Wisdom from God's Holy Word

Now faith is the reality of what is hoped for, the proof of what is not seen.

Hebrews 11:1 HCSB

Now without faith it is impossible to please God, for the one who draws near to Him must believe that He exists and rewards those who seek Him.

Hebrews 11:6 HCSB

For we walk by faith, not by sight.

2 Corinthians 5:7 HCSB

If you do not stand firm in your faith, then you will not stand at all.

Isaiah 7:9 HCSB

More Great Ideas

Just as our faith strengthens our prayer life, so do our prayers deepen our faith. Let us pray often, starting today, for a deeper, more powerful faith.

Shirley Dobson

Faith does not concern itself with the entire journey. One step is enough.

Mrs. Charles E. Cowman

Grace calls you to get up, throw off your blanket of helplessness, and to move on through life in faith.

Kay Arthur

Faith is seeing light with the eyes of your heart, when the eyes of your body see only darkness.

Barbara Johnson

Sometimes the very essence of faith is trusting God in the midst of things He knows good and well we cannot comprehend.

Beth Moore

He wants us to have a faith
that does not complain while
waiting, but rejoices because
we know our times are in
His hands—nail-scarred hands
that labor for our highest good.

—

Kay Arthur

Today's Timely Tip

Faith in God is contagious, and when it comes to your family's spiritual journey, no one's faith is more contagious than yours! Act, pray, praise, and trust God with the certain knowledge that every member of your family is watching . . . carefully!

Today's Prayer

Dear Lord, help me to be a woman of faith. Help me to remember that You are always near and that You can overcome any challenge. With Your love and Your power, Lord, I can live courageously and faithfully today and every day. Amen

DAY 13

STRENGTH FOR THE JOURNEY

And He said to me,
"My grace is sufficient for you,
for My strength is made perfect in weakness."

—

2 Corinthians 12:9 NKJV

W here do you go to find strength? The gym? The health food store? The espresso bar? There's a better source of strength, of course, and that source is God. He is a never-ending source of strength and courage if you call upon Him.

Are you an energized Christian? You should be. But if you're not, you must seek strength and renewal from the source that will never fail: that source, of course, is your Heavenly Father. And rest assured—when you sincerely petition Him, He will give you all the strength you need to live victoriously for Him.

Have you "tapped in" to the power of God? Have you turned your life and your heart over to Him, or are you muddling along under your own power? The answer to this question will determine the quality of your life here on earth and the destiny of your life throughout all eternity. So start tapping in—and remember that when it comes to strength, God is the Ultimate Source.

Wisdom from God's Holy Word

You, therefore, my child, be strong in the grace that is in Christ Jesus.

2 Timothy 2:1 HCSB

The Lord is my strength and my song; He has become my salvation.

Exodus 15:2 HCSB

He gives strength to the weary and strengthens the powerless.

Isaiah 40:29 HCSB

But those who wait on the Lord shall renew their strength; they shall mount up with wings like eagles, they shall run and not be weary, they shall walk and not faint.

Isaiah 40:31 NKJV

Finally, be strengthened by the Lord and by His vast strength.

Ephesians 6:10 HCSB

More Great Ideas

Worry does not empty tomorrow of its sorrow; it empties today of its strength.

Corrie ten Boom

One reason so much American Christianity is a mile wide and an inch deep is that Christians are simply tired. Sometimes you need to kick back and rest for Jesus' sake.

Dennis Swanberg

God does not dispense strength and encouragement like a druggist fills your prescription. The Lord doesn't promise to give us something to take so we can handle our weary moments. He promises us Himself. That is all. And that is enough.

Charles Swindoll

Sometimes I think spiritual and physical strength is like manna: you get just what you need for the day, no more.

Suzanne Dale Ezell

No matter how heavy
the burden, daily strength is
given, so I expect we need not
give ourselves any concern as
to what the outcome will be.
We must simply go forward.

—

Annie Armstrong

Today's Timely Tip

Feeling exhausted? Try this: Start getting more sleep each night; begin a program of regular, sensible exercise; avoid harmful food and drink; and turn your problems over to God . . . and the greatest of these is "turn your problems over to God."

Today's Prayer

Dear Heavenly Father, You are my strength and my protector. When I am troubled, You comfort me. When I am discouraged, You lift me up. When I am afraid, You deliver me. Let me turn to You, Lord, when I am weak. In times of adversity, let me trust Your plan, Lord, and whatever my circumstances, let me look to You for my strength and my salvation. Amen

PRIORITIES FOR THE JOURNEY

He said to them all, "If anyone desires to come after Me, let him deny himself, and take up his cross daily, and follow Me. For whoever desires to save his life will lose it, but whoever loses his life for My sake will save it."

—

Luke 9:23-24 NKJV

"First things first." These words are easy to speak but hard to put into practice. For busy women living in a demanding world, placing first things first can be difficult indeed. Why? Because so many people are expecting so many things from us!

If you're having trouble prioritizing your day, perhaps you've been trying to organize your life according to your own plans, not God's. A better strategy, of course, is to take your daily obligations and place them in the hands of the One who created you. To do so, you must prioritize your day according to God's commandments, and you must seek His will and His wisdom in all matters. Then, you can face the day with the assurance that the same God who created our universe out of nothingness will help you place first things first in your own life.

Do you feel overwhelmed or confused? Turn the concerns of this day over to God—prayerfully, earnestly, and often. Then listen for His answer . . . and trust the answer He gives.

Wisdom from God's Holy Word

For where your treasure is, there your heart will be also.

Luke 12:34 HCSB

And I pray this: that your love will keep on growing in knowledge and every kind of discernment, so that you can determine what really matters and can be pure and blameless in the day of Christ.

Philippians 1:9 HCSB

Now it happened as they went that He entered a certain village; and a certain woman named Martha welcomed Him into her house. And she had a sister called Mary, who also sat at Jesus' feet and heard His word. But Martha was distracted with much serving, and she approached Him and said, "Lord, do You not care that my sister has left me to serve alone? Therefore tell her to help me." And Jesus answered and said to her, "Martha, Martha, you are worried and troubled about many things. But one thing is needed, and Mary has chosen that good part, which will not be taken away from her."

Luke 10:38-42 NKJV

91

More Great Ideas

Sin is largely a matter of mistaken priorities. Any sin in us that is cherished, hidden, and not confessed will cut the nerve center of our faith.

Catherine Marshall

Have you prayed about your resources lately? Find out how God wants you to use your time and your money. No matter what it costs, forsake all that is not of God.

Kay Arthur

Great relief and satisfaction can come from seeking God's priorities for us in each season, discerning what is "best" in the midst of many noble opportunities, and pouring our most excellent energies into those things.

Beth Moore

We set our eyes on the finish line, forgetting the past, and straining toward the mark of spiritual maturity and fruitfulness.

Vonette Bright

The things that matter most
in this world can never
be held in your hand.

—

Gloria Gaither

Today's Timely Tip

Unless you put first things first, you're bound to finish last. And don't forget that putting first things first means God first and family next.

Today's Prayer

Dear Lord, today is a new day. Help me finish the important tasks first, even if those tasks are unpleasant. Don't let me put off until tomorrow what I should do today. Amen

DAY 15

HE RENEWS

*I will give you a new heart
and put a new spirit within you.*

—

Ezekiel 36:26 HCSB

For busy women living in a fast-paced 21st-century world, life may seem like a merry-go-round that never stops turning. If that description seems to fit your life, then you may find yourself running short of patience, or strength, or both. If you're feeling tired or discouraged, there is a source from which you can draw the power needed to recharge your spiritual batteries. That source is God.

Are you exhausted or troubled? Turn your heart toward God in prayer. Are you weak or worried? Take the time—or, more accurately, make the time—to delve deeply into God's Holy Word. Are you spiritually depleted? Call upon fellow believers to support you, and call upon Christ to renew your spirit and your life. When you do, you'll discover that the Creator of the universe stands always ready and always able to create a new sense of wonderment and joy in you.

Wisdom from God's Holy Word

But may the God of all grace, who called us to His eternal glory by Christ Jesus, after you have suffered a while, perfect, establish, strengthen, and settle you.

1 Peter 5:10 NKJV

Finally, brothers, rejoice. Be restored, be encouraged, be of the same mind, be at peace, and the God of love and peace will be with you.

2 Corinthians 13:11 HCSB

But those who wait on the Lord shall renew their strength; they shall mount up with wings like eagles, they shall run and not be weary, they shall walk and not faint.

Isaiah 40:31 NKJV

Therefore if anyone is in Christ, he is a new creature; the old things passed away; behold, new things have come.

2 Corinthians 5:17 HCSB

More Great Ideas

God specializes in things fresh and firsthand. His plans for you this year may outshine those of the past. He's prepared to fill your days with reasons to give Him praise.

Joni Eareckson Tada

Whoever you are, whatever your condition or circumstance, whatever your past or problem, Jesus can restore you to wholeness.

Anne Graham Lotz

Repentance removes old sins and wrong attitudes, and it opens the way for the Holy Spirit to restore our spiritual health.

Shirley Dobson

He is the God of wholeness and restoration.

Stormie Omartian

Troubles we bear trustfully can bring us a fresh vision of God and a new outlook on life, an outlook of peace and hope.

Billy Graham

The amazing thing about Jesus
is that He doesn't just
patch up our lives;
He gives us a brand new sheet,
a clean slate to start over,
all new.

—

Gloria Gaither

Today's Timely Tip

Do you need time for yourself? Take it. Ruth Bell Graham observed, "It is important that we take time out for ourselves—for relaxation, for refreshment." Enough said.

Today's Prayer

Lord, I am an imperfect woman. Because my faith is limited, I may become overwhelmed by the demands of the day. When I feel tired or discouraged, renew my strength. When I am worried, let me turn my thoughts and my prayers to You. Let me trust Your promises, Dear Lord, and let me accept Your unending love, now and forever. Amen

DAY 16

CONTINUING
TO GROW

*For this reason also, since the day we heard this,
we haven't stopped praying for you.
We are asking that you may be filled with
the knowledge of His will in all wisdom and
spiritual understanding.*

—

Colossians 1:9 HCSB

When will you be a "fully-grown" Christian? Hopefully never—or at least not until you arrive in heaven! As a believer, you're never "fully grown"; you always have the potential to keep growing.

Many of life's most important lessons are painful to learn, but spiritual growth need not take place only in times of pain and hardship. Whatever your circumstances, God is always standing at the door; whenever you are ready to reach out to Him, He will answer.

In those quiet moments when you open your heart to God, the One who made you keeps remaking you. He gives you direction, perspective, wisdom, and courage. And, the appropriate moment to accept those spiritual gifts is always the present one.

Would you like a time-tested formula for spiritual growth? Here it is: keep studying God's Word, keep obeying His commandments, keep praying (and listening for answers), and seek to live in the center of God's will. When you do, you will never be a "stagnant" believer. You will, instead, be a growing Christian.

Wisdom from God's Holy Word

But grow in the grace and knowledge of our Lord and Savior Jesus Christ. To Him be the glory both now and to the day of eternity.

2 Peter 3:18 HCSB

I want their hearts to be encouraged and joined together in love, so that they may have all the riches of assured understanding, and have the knowledge of God's mystery—Christ.

Colossians 2:2 HCSB

For You, O God, have tested us; You have refined us as silver is refined. You brought us into the net; You laid affliction on our backs. You have caused men to ride over our heads; we went through fire and through water; but You brought us out to rich fulfillment.

Psalm 66:10–12 NKJV

More Great Ideas

We set our eyes on the finish line, forgetting the past, and straining toward the mark of spiritual maturity and fruitfulness.

Vonette Bright

We look at our burdens and heavy loads, and we shrink from them. But, if we lift them and bind them about our hearts, they become wings, and on them we can rise and soar toward God.

Mrs. Charles E. Cowman

If all struggles and sufferings were eliminated, the spirit would no more reach maturity than would the child.

Elisabeth Elliot

Growth in depth and strength and consistency and fruitfulness and ultimately in Christlikeness is only possible when the winds of life are contrary to personal comfort.

Anne Graham Lotz

As we spend time reading,
applying, and obeying
our Bibles, the Spirit of Truth
Who is also the Spirit of Jesus
increasingly reveals
Jesus to us.

—

Anne Graham Lotz

Today's Timely Tip

Spiritual maturity is a journey, not a destination. A growing relationship with God should be your highest priority.

Today's Prayer

Lord, help me to keep growing spiritually and emotionally. Let me live according to Your Word, and let me grow in my faith every day that I live. Amen

BE STILL MY SOUL

Be still, and know that I am God . . . .

—

Psalm 46:10 KJV

Are you so busy that you rush through the day with scarcely a single moment for quiet contemplation and prayer? If so, it's time to reorder your priorities.

We live in a noisy world, a world filled with distractions, frustrations, and complications. But if we allow the distractions of a clamorous world to separate us from God's peace, we do ourselves a profound disservice. If we are to maintain righteous minds and compassionate hearts, we must take time each day for prayer and for meditation. We must make ourselves still in the presence of our Creator. We must quiet our minds and our hearts so that we might sense God's will, God's love, and God's Son.

Has the busy pace of life robbed you of the peace that might otherwise be yours through Jesus Christ? Nothing is more important than the time you spend with your Savior. So be still and claim the inner peace that is your spiritual birthright: the peace of Jesus Christ. It is offered freely; it has been paid for in full; it is yours for the asking. So ask. And then share.

Wisdom from God's Holy Word

Be silent before Me.

Isaiah 41:1 HCSB

Be silent before the Lord and wait expectantly for Him.

Psalm 37:7 HCSB

Truly my soul silently waits for God; from Him comes my salvation.

Psalm 62:1 NKJV

My soul, wait silently for God alone, for my expectation is from Him.

Psalm 62:5 NKJV

But those who wait on the Lord shall renew their strength; they shall mount up with wings like eagles, they shall run and not be weary, they shall walk and not faint.

Isaiah 40:31 NKJV

More Great Ideas

When we are in the presence of God, removed from distractions, we are able to hear
him more clearly, and a secure environment
has been established for the young and broken
places in our hearts to surface.

John Eldredge

The world is full of noise. Might we not set
ourselves to learn silence, stillness, solitude?

Elisabeth Elliot

Because Jesus Christ is our Great High Priest,
not only can we approach God without a human "go-between," we can also hear and learn
from God in some sacred moments without
one.

Beth Moore

Let your loneliness be transformed into a holy
aloneness. Sit still before the Lord. Remember
Naomi's word to Ruth: "Sit still, my daughter,
until you see how the matter will fall."

Elisabeth Elliot

Let this be your chief object in
prayer, to realize the presence
of your Heavenly Father.
Let your watchword be:
Alone with God.

—

Andrew Murray

Today's Timely Tip

Try this experiment: the next time you're driving alone in your automobile, do so without the radio, CDs, or cell phones. And then, have a quiet talk with God about His plans for your life. You may be surprised to discover that sometimes the most important answers are the ones you receive in silence.

Today's Prayer

Dear Lord, let me be still before You. When I am hurried or distracted, slow me down and redirect my thoughts. When I am confused, give me perspective. Keep me mindful, Father, that You are always with me. And let me sense Your presence today, tomorrow, and forever. Amen

HE WANTS YOU TO SERVE

Worship the Lord your God and . . .
serve Him only.

—

Matthew 4:10 HCSB

We live in a world that glorifies power, prestige, fame, and money. But the words of Jesus teach us that the most esteemed men and women in this world are not the self-congratulatory leaders of society but are instead the humblest of servants.

Are you willing to become a humble servant for Christ? Are you willing to pitch in and make the world a better place, or are you determined to keep all your blessings to yourself. The answers to these questions will determine the quantity and the quality of the service you render to God and to His children.

Today, you may feel the temptation to take more than you give. You may be tempted to withhold your generosity. Or you may be tempted to build yourself up in the eyes of your friends. Resist those temptations. Instead, serve your friends quietly and without fanfare. Find a need and fill it . . . humbly. Lend a helping hand . . . anonymously. Share a word of kindness . . . with quiet sincerity. As you go about your daily activities, remember that the Savior of all humanity made Himself a servant, and we, as His followers, must do no less.

Wisdom from God's Holy Word

A person should consider us in this way: as servants of Christ and managers of God's mysteries. In this regard, it is expected of managers that each one be found faithful.

1 Corinthians 4:1-2 HCSB

If they serve Him obediently, they will end their days in prosperity and their years in happiness.

Job 36:11 HCSB

We must do the works of Him who sent Me while it is day. Night is coming when no one can work.

John 9:4 HCSB

Serve the Lord with gladness.

Psalm 100:2 HCSB

If anyone serves Me, let him follow Me; and where I am, there My servant will be also. If anyone serves Me, him My Father will honor.

John 12:26 NKJV

More Great Ideas

In the very place where God has put us, whatever its limitations, whatever kind of work it may be, we may indeed serve the Lord Christ.

Elisabeth Elliot

Doing something positive toward another person is a practical approach to feeling good about yourself.

Barbara Johnson

Through our service to others, God wants to influence our world for Him.

Vonette Bright

God wants us to serve Him with a willing spirit, one that would choose no other way.

Beth Moore

If you want to discover your spiritual gifts, start obeying God. As you serve Him, you will find that He has given you the gifts that are necessary to follow through in obedience.

Anne Graham Lotz

We have to serve God
in His way,
not in ours.

—

St. Teresa of Avila

Today's Timely Tip

Jesus was a servant, and if you want to follow Him, you must be a servant, too—even when service requires sacrifice.

Today's Prayer

Dear Lord, in weak moments, I seek to build myself up by placing myself ahead of others. But Your commandment, Father, is that I become a humble servant to those who need my encouragement, my help, and my love. Create in me a servant's heart. And, let me be a woman who follows in the footsteps of Your Son Jesus who taught us by example that to be great in Your eyes, Lord, is to serve others humbly, faithfully, and lovingly. Amen

THE IMPORTANCE OF WORSHIP

But an hour is coming, and is now here,
when the true worshipers will worship the Father
in spirit and truth. Yes, the Father wants such
people to worship Him. God is Spirit,
and those who worship Him must
worship in spirit and truth.

—

John 4:23-24 HCSB

All of humanity is engaged in worship. The question is not *whether* we worship, but *what* we worship. Wise men and women choose to worship God. When they do, they are blessed with a plentiful harvest of joy, peace, and abundance. Other people choose to distance themselves from God by foolishly worshiping things that are intended to bring personal gratification but not spiritual gratification. Such choices often have tragic consequences.

If we place our love for material possessions above our love for God—or if we yield to the countless temptations of this world—we find ourselves engaged in a struggle between good and evil. Our responses to these struggles have implications that echo throughout our families and throughout our communities.

How can we ensure that we cast our lot with God? We do so, in part, by the practice of regular, purposeful worship in the company of fellow believers. When we worship God faithfully and fervently, we are blessed. When we fail to worship God, for whatever reason, we forfeit the spiritual gifts that He intends for us.

We must worship our Heavenly Father, not just with our words, but also with our deeds. We must honor Him, praise Him, and obey Him. As we seek to find purpose and meaning for our lives, we must first seek His purpose and His will. For believers, God comes first. Always first.

Wisdom from God's Holy Word

So that at the name of Jesus every knee should bow—of those who are in heaven and on earth and under the earth—and every tongue should confess that Jesus Christ is Lord, to the glory of God the Father.

Philippians 2:10-11 HCSB

Worship the Lord your God and . . . serve Him only.

Matthew 4:10 HCSB

If anyone is thirsty, he should come to Me and drink!

John 7:37 HCSB

More Great Ideas

God asks that we worship Him with our concentrated minds as well as with our wills and emotions. A divided and scattered mind is not effective.

Catherine Marshall

Spiritual worship comes from our very core and is fueled by an awesome reverence and desire for God.

Beth Moore

To worship Him in truth means to worship Him honestly, without hypocrisy, standing open and transparent before Him.

Anne Graham Lotz

God actually delights in and pursues our worship (Proverbs 15:8 & John 4:23).

Shirley Dobson

In the sanctuary, we discover beauty: the beauty of His presence.

Kay Arthur

Spiritual worship is focusing
all we are on all He is.

—

Beth Moore

Today's Timely Tip

The best way to worship God . . . is to worship Him sincerely and often.

Today's Prayer

Lord, let me worship You every day of my life, and let me discover the peace that can be mine when I welcome You into my heart. Amen

DETOURS ON THE JOURNEY

We are pressured in every way but not crushed;
we are perplexed but not in despair.

—

2 Corinthians 4:8 HCSB

W omen of every generation have experienced adversity, and this generation is no different. But, today's women face challenges that previous generations could have scarcely imagined. Thankfully, although the world continues to change, God's love remains constant. And, He remains ready to comfort us and strengthen us whenever we turn to Him.

Psalm 147 promises, "He heals the brokenhearted, and binds their wounds" (v. 3). When we are troubled, we must call upon God, and, in His own time and according to His own plan, He will heal us.

If you are like most women, it is simply a fact of life: from time to time, you worry. You worry about health, about finances, about safety, about relationships, about family, and about countless other challenges of life, some great and some small. Where is the best place to take your worries? Take them to God. Take your troubles to Him, and your fears, and your sorrows. Seek protection from the One who cannot be moved.

Wisdom from God's Holy Word,

I called to the Lord in my distress; I called to my God. From His temple He heard my voice.

2 Samuel 22:7 HCSB

Consider it a great joy, my brothers, whenever you experience various trials, knowing that the testing of your faith produces endurance. But endurance must do its complete work, so that you may be mature and complete, lacking nothing.

James 1:2-4 HCSB

When you are in distress and all these things have happened to you, you will return to the Lord your God in later days and obey Him. He will not leave you, destroy you, or forget the covenant with your fathers that He swore to them by oath, because the Lord your God is a compassionate God.

Deuteronomy 4:30-31 HCSB

But as for you, you meant evil against me; but God meant it for good, in order to bring it about as it is this day, to save many people alive.

Genesis 50:20 NKJV

127

More Great Ideas

God will never let you sink under your circumstances. He always provides a safety net and His love always encircles.

Barbara Johnson

Measure the size of the obstacles against the size of God.

Beth Moore

If all struggles and sufferings were eliminated, the spirit would no more reach maturity than would the child.

Elisabeth Elliot

Faith is a strong power, mastering any difficulty in the strength of the Lord who made heaven and earth.

Corrie ten Boom

When faced with adversity the Christian woman comforts herself with the knowledge that all of life's events are in the hands of God.

Vonette Bright

Every misfortune, every failure,
every loss may be transformed.
God has the power to
transform all misfortunes
into "God-sends."

—

Mrs. Charles E. Cowman

Today's Timely Tip

If you're facing big-time adversity, don't hit the panic button and don't keep everything bottled up inside. Instead of going underground, talk things over with your husband, with your friends, with your pastor, and if necessary, with a trained counselor. When it comes to navigating the stormy seas of life, second, third, fourth, or even fifth opinions can sometimes be helpful.

Today's Prayer

Dear Heavenly Father, when I am troubled, You heal me. When I am afraid, You protect me. When I am discouraged, You lift me up. You are my unending source of strength, Lord; let me turn to You when I am weak. In times of adversity, let me trust Your plan and Your will for my life. And whatever my circumstances, Lord, let me always give the thanks and the glory to You. Amen

DAY 21

THIS IS THE DAY

This is the day the LORD has made;
we will rejoice and be glad in it.

—

Psalm 118:24 NKJV

The familiar words of Psalm 118:24 remind us of a profound yet simple truth: God created this day, and it's up to each of us to rejoice and to be grateful.

For Christians, every day begins and ends with God and His Son. Christ came to this earth to give us abundant life and eternal salvation. We give thanks to our Maker when we treasure each day and use it to the fullest.

This day is a gift from God. How will you use it? Will you celebrate God's gifts and obey His commandments? Will you share words of encouragement and hope with all who cross your path? Will you share the Good News of the risen Christ? Will you trust in the Father and praise His glorious handiwork? The answer to these questions will determine, to a surprising extent, the direction and the quality of your day.

So whatever this day holds for you, begin it and end it with God as your partner and Christ as your Savior. And throughout the day, give thanks to the One who created you and saved you. God's love for you is infinite. Accept it joyously and be thankful.

Wisdom from God's Holy Word

Working together with Him, we also appeal to you: "Don't receive God's grace in vain." For He says: In an acceptable time, I heard you, and in the day of salvation, I helped you. Look, now is the acceptable time; look, now is the day of salvation.

2 Corinthians 6:1-2 HCSB

I must work the works of Him who sent Me while it is day; the night is coming when no one can work.

John 9:4 NKJV

Therefore, get your minds ready for action, being self-disciplined, and set your hope completely on the grace to be brought to you at the revelation of Jesus Christ.

1 Peter 1:13 HCSB

But encourage each other daily, while it is still called today, so that none of you is hardened by sin's deception.

Hebrews 3:13 HCSB

More Great Ideas

Yesterday is the tomb of time, and tomorrow is the womb of time. Only now is yours.

R. G. Lee

Christ is the secret, the source, the substance, the center, and the circumference of all true and lasting gladness.

Mrs. Charles E. Cowman

When the dream of our heart is one that God has planted there, a strange happiness flows into us. At that moment, all of the spiritual resources of the universe are released to help us. Our praying is then at one with the will of God and becomes a channel for the Creator's purposes for us and our world.

Catherine Marshall

If you can forgive the person you were, accept the person you are, and believe in the person you will become, you are headed for joy. So celebrate your life.

Barbara Johnson

Joy is the keynote of
the Christian life. It is not
something that happens.
It is a gift, given to us in
the coming of Christ.

—

Elisabeth Elliot

Today's Timely Tip

If you don't feel like celebrating, start counting your blessings. Before long, you'll realize that you have plenty of reasons to celebrate.

Today's Prayer

Dear Lord, You have given me another day of life; let me celebrate this day, and let me use it according to Your plan. I come to You today with faith in my heart and praise on my lips. I praise You, Father, for the gift of life and for the friends and family members who make my life rich. Enable me to live each moment to the fullest, totally involved in Your will. Amen

MAINTAINING PERSPECTIVE

Make your own attitude that of Christ Jesus.

—

Philippians 2:5 HCSB

Sometimes, amid the demands of daily life, we lose perspective. Life seems out of balance, and the pressures of everyday living seem overwhelming. What's needed is a fresh perspective, a restored sense of balance and God.

If a temporary loss of perspective has left you worried, exhausted, or both, it's time to readjust your thought patterns. Negative thoughts are habit-forming; thankfully, so are positive ones. With practice, you can form the habit of focusing on God's priorities and your possibilities. When you do, you'll soon discover that you will spend less time fretting about your challenges and more time praising God for His gifts.

When you call upon the Lord and prayerfully seek His will, He will give you wisdom and perspective. When you make God's priorities your priorities, He will direct your steps and calm your fears. So today and every day hereafter, pray for a sense of balance and perspective. And remember: your thoughts are intensely powerful things, so handle them with care.

Wisdom from God's Holy Word

Finally brothers, whatever is true, whatever is honorable, whatever is just, whatever is pure, whatever is lovely, whatever is commendable—if there is any moral excellence and if there is any praise—dwell on these things.

Philippians 4:8 HCSB

Let this mind be in you which was also in Christ Jesus, who, being in the form of God, did not consider it robbery to be equal with God, but made Himself of no reputation, taking the form of a bondservant, and coming in the likeness of men. And being found in appearance as a man, He humbled Himself and became obedient to the point of death, even the death of the cross.

Philippians 2:5-8 NKJV

For the word of God is living and powerful, and sharper than any two-edged sword, piercing even to the division of soul and spirit, and of joints and marrow, and is a discerner of the thoughts and intents of the heart.

Hebrews 4:12 NKJV

More Great Ideas

Earthly fears are no fears at all. Answer the big questions of eternity, and the little questions of life fall into perspective.

Max Lucado

Instead of being frustrated and overwhelmed by all that is going on in our world, go to the Lord and ask Him to give you His eternal perspective.

Kay Arthur

Attitude is the mind's paintbrush; it can color any situation.

Barbara Johnson

When the dream of our heart is one that God has planted there, a strange happiness flows into us. At that moment, all of the spiritual resources of the universe are released to help us. Our praying is then at one with the will of God and becomes a channel for the Creator's purposes for us and our world.

Catherine Marshall

Joy is the direct result of
having God's perspective on
our daily lives and the effect of
loving our Lord enough
to obey His commands and
trust His promises.

—

Bill Bright

Today's Timely Tip

Keep things in perspective. Your life is an integral part of God's grand plan. So don't become unduly upset over the minor inconveniences of life, and don't worry too much about today's setbacks—they're temporary.

Today's Prayer

Dear Lord, give me wisdom and perspective. Guide me according to Your plans for my life and according to Your commandments. And keep me mindful, dear Lord, that Your truth is—and will forever be—the ultimate truth. Amen

ACCEPTING GOD'S ABUNDANCE

*I am come that they might have life,
and that they might have it more abundantly.*

—

John 10:10 KJV

The familiar words of John 10:10 should serve as a daily reminder: Christ came to this earth so that we might experience His abundance, His love, and His gift of eternal life. But Christ does not force Himself upon us; we must claim His gifts for ourselves.

Every woman knows that some days are so busy and so hurried that abundance seems a distant promise. It is not. Every day, we can claim the spiritual abundance that God promises for our lives . . . and we should.

Thomas Brooks spoke for believers of every generation when he observed, "Christ is the sun, and all the watches of our lives should be set by the dial of his motion." Christ, indeed, is the ultimate Savior of mankind and the personal Savior of those who believe in Him. As His servants, we should place Him at the very center of our lives. And, every day that God gives us breath, we should share Christ's love and His abundance with a world that needs both.

Wisdom from God's Holy Word

Until now you have asked for nothing in My name. Ask and you will receive, that your joy may be complete.

John 16:24 HCSB

And God is able to make every grace overflow to you, so that in every way, always having everything you need, you may excel in every good work.

2 Corinthians 9:8 HCSB

My cup runs over. Surely goodness and mercy shall follow me all the days of my life; and I will dwell in the house of the Lord forever.

Psalm 23:5-6 NKJV

And He said to them, "Take heed and beware of covetousness, for one's life does not consist in the abundance of the things he possesses."

Luke 12:15 NKJV

More Great Ideas

Yes, we were created for His holy pleasure, but we will ultimately—if not immediately—find much pleasure in His pleasure.

Beth Moore

It would be wrong to have a "poverty complex," for to think ourselves paupers is to deny either the King's riches or to deny our being His children.

Catherine Marshall

God's riches are beyond anything we could ask or even dare to imagine! If my life gets gooey and stale, I have no excuse.

Barbara Johnson

God is the giver, and we are the receivers. And His richest gifts are bestowed not upon those who do the greatest things, but upon those who accept His abundance and His grace.

Hannah Whitall Smith

Whatever may be
our circumstances in life,
may each one of us really
believe that by way of
the Throne we have
unlimited power.

—

Annie Armstrong

Today's Timely Tip

When Jesus talked about abundance, was He talking about money? Nope. When Christ talked about abundance, He was concerned with people's spiritual well-being, not their financial well-being. That's a lesson that you must learn . . . and it's a lesson that you must share with your child.

Today's Prayer

Dear Lord, thank You for the joyful, abundant life that is mine through Christ Jesus. Guide me according to Your will, and help me become a woman whose life is a worthy example to others. Give me courage, Lord, to claim the spiritual riches that You have promised, and show me Your plan for my life, today and forever. Amen

DAY 24

THANKSGIVING NOW

In everything give thanks;
for this is the will of God in Christ Jesus for you.

—

1 Thessalonians 5:18 NKJV

As busy women caught up in the inevitable demands of everyday life, we sometimes fail to pause and thank our Creator for the countless blessings He has bestowed upon us. And that's unfortunate because, as believing Christians, we are blessed beyond measure.

God sent His only Son to die for our sins. And, God has given us the priceless gifts of eternal love and eternal life. We, in turn, are instructed to approach our Heavenly Father with reverence and thanksgiving.

When we slow down and express our gratitude to the One who made us, we enrich our own lives and the lives of those around us. Thanksgiving should become a habit, a regular part of our daily routines. Yes, God has blessed us beyond measure, and we owe Him everything, including our eternal praise.

Wisdom from God's Holy Word

Thanks be to God for His indescribable gift.

2 Corinthians 9:15 HCSB

Therefore as you have received Christ Jesus the Lord, walk in Him, rooted and built up in Him and established in the faith, just as you were taught, and overflowing with thankfulness.

Colossians 2:6-7 HCSB

Enter into His gates with thanksgiving, and into His courts with praise. Be thankful to Him, and bless His name. For the Lord is good; His mercy is everlasting, and His truth endures to all generations.

Psalm 100:4-5 NKJV

And whatever you do, in word or in deed, do everything in the name of the Lord Jesus, giving thanks to God the Father through Him.

Colossians 3:17 HCSB

More Great Ideas

Thanksgiving or complaining—these words express two contrastive attitudes of the souls of God's children in regard to His dealings with them. The soul that gives thanks can find comfort in everything; the soul that complains can find comfort in nothing.

Hannah Whitall Smith

The act of thanksgiving is a demonstration of the fact that you are going to trust and believe God.

Kay Arthur

God is worthy of our praise and is pleased when we come before Him with thanksgiving.

Shirley Dobson

Do you know that if at birth I had been able to make one petition, it would have been that I should be born blind? Because, when I get to heaven, the first face that shall ever gladden my sight will be that of my Savior!

Fanny Crosby

God is in control, and
therefore in everything
I can give thanks,
not because of the situation,
but because of the One who
directs and rules over it.

—

Kay Arthur

Today's Timely Tip

When is the best time to say "thanks" to God? Any time. God never takes a vacation, and He's always ready to hear from you. So what are you waiting for?

Today's Prayer

Dear Lord, I'm really thankful for all the good things I have. Today I will show You how grateful I am, not only by the words that I speak, but also by the way that I act. Amen

THE RIGHT KIND OF EXAMPLE

*You should be an example to the believers
in speech, in conduct, in love,
in faith, in purity.*

—

1 Timothy 4:12 HCSB

Whether we like it or not, all of us are role models. Our friends and family members watch our actions and, as followers of Christ, we are obliged to act accordingly.

What kind of example are you? Are you the kind of woman whose life serves as a genuine example of righteousness? Are you a woman whose behavior serves as a positive role model for young people? Are you the kind of woman whose actions, day in and day out, are based upon kindness, faithfulness, and a love for the Lord? If so, you are not only blessed by God, but you are also a powerful force for good in a world that desperately needs positive influences such as yours.

Corrie ten Boom advised, "Don't worry about what you do not understand. Worry about what you do understand in the Bible but do not live by." And that's sound advice because our families and friends are watching . . . and so, for that matter, is God.

Wisdom from God's Holy Word

Do everything without grumbling and arguing, so that you may be blameless and pure.

Philippians 2:14–15 HCSB

Set an example of good works yourself, with integrity and dignity in your teaching.

Titus 2:7 HCSB

For the kingdom of God is not in talk but in power.

1 Corinthians 4:20 HCSB

Therefore since we also have such a large cloud of witnesses surrounding us, let us lay aside every weight and the sin that so easily ensnares us, and run with endurance the race that lies before us.

Hebrews 12:1 HCSB

You are the light of the world. A city situated on a hill cannot be hidden.

Matthew 5:14 HCSB

More Great Ideas

Heredity does not equip a child with proper attitudes; children learn what they are taught. We cannot expect proper behavior to appear magically.

James Dobson

Living life with a consistent spiritual walk deeply influences those we love most.

Vonette Bright

Each one of us is God's special work of art. Through us, He teaches and inspires, delights and encourages, informs and uplifts all those who view our lives. God, the master artist, is most concerned about expressing Himself— His thoughts and His intentions—through what He paints in our character. . . . [He] wants to paint a beautiful portrait of His Son in and through your life. A painting like no other in all of time.

Joni Eareckson Tada

Study the Bible and observe
how the persons behaved and
how God dealt with them.
There is explicit teaching
on every condition of life.

—

Corrie ten Boom

Today's Timely Tip

Living Your Life and Shining Your Light: As a Christian, the most important light you shine is the light that your own life shines on the lives of others. May your light shine brightly, righteously, obediently, and eternally!

Today's Prayer

Dear Lord, help me be a worthy example to my friends and to my family. Let the things that I say and the things that I do show everyone what it means to be a follower of Your Son. Amen

DAY 26

ENCOURAGEMENT FOR THE JOURNEY

I want their hearts to be encouraged and joined together in love, so that they may have all the riches of assured understanding, and have the knowledge of God's mystery—Christ.

—

Colossians 2:2 HCSB

A re you a woman who is a continuing source of encouragement to your family and friends? Hopefully so. After all, one of the reasons that God put you here is to serve and encourage other people—starting with your family.

In his letter to the Ephesians, Paul writes, "Do not let any unwholesome talk come out of your mouths, but only what is helpful for building others up according to their needs, that it may benefit those who listen" (4:29 NIV). This passage reminds us that, as Christians, we are instructed to choose our words carefully so as to build others up through wholesome, honest encouragement. How can we build others up? By celebrating their victories and their accomplishments. As the old saying goes, "When someone does something good, applaud—you'll make two people happy."

Today, look for the good in others and celebrate the good that you find. When you do, you'll be a powerful force of encouragement in your corner of the world . . . and a worthy servant to your God.

Wisdom from God's Holy Word

Carry one another's burdens; in this way you will fulfill the law of Christ.

Galatians 6:2 HCSB

But encourage each other daily, while it is still called today, so that none of you is hardened by sin's deception.

Hebrews 3:13 HCSB

And let us be concerned about one another in order to promote love and good works.

Hebrews 10:24 HCSB

Anxiety in a man's heart weighs it down, but a good word cheers it up.

Proverbs 12:25 HCSB

So then, we must pursue what promotes peace and what builds up one another.

Romans 14:19 HCSB

More Great Ideas

The glory of friendship is not the outstretched hand, or the kindly smile, or the joy of companionship. It is the spiritual inspiration that comes to one when he discovers that someone else believes in him and is willing to trust him with his friendship.

Corrie ten Boom

Always stay connected to people and seek out things that bring you joy. Dream with abandon. Pray confidently.

Barbara Johnson

Don't forget that a single sentence, spoken at the right moment, can change somebody's whole perspective on life. A little encouragement can go a long, long way.

Marie T. Freeman

A single word,
if spoken in a friendly spirit,
may be sufficient to turn one
from dangerous error.

—

Fanny Crosby

Today's Timely Tip

Encouragement is contagious. You can't lift other people up without lifting yourself up, too.

Today's Prayer

Dear Heavenly Father, because I am Your child, I am blessed. You have loved me eternally, cared for me faithfully, and saved me through the gift of Your Son Jesus. Just as You have lifted me up, Lord, let me lift up others in a spirit of encouragement and optimism and hope. And, if I can help a fellow traveler, even in a small way, Dear Lord, may the glory be Yours. Amen

ABOVE AND BEYOND WORRY

*Don't worry about your life, what you will eat
or what you will drink; or about your body,
what you will wear. Isn't life more than
food and the body more than clothing?*

—

Matthew 6:25 HCSB

I f you are like most women, it is simply a fact of life: from time to time, you worry. You worry about health, about finances, about safety, about relationships, about family, and about countless other challenges of life, some great and some small. Where is the best place to take your worries? Take them to God. Take your troubles to Him, and your fears, and your sorrows.

Barbara Johnson correctly observed, "Worry is the senseless process of cluttering up tomorrow's opportunities with leftover problems from today." So if you'd like to make the most out of this day (and every one hereafter), turn your worries over to a Power greater than yourself . . . and spend your valuable time and energy solving the problems you can fix . . . while trusting God to do the rest.

Wisdom from God's Holy Word

Don't worry about anything, but in everything, through prayer and petition with thanksgiving, let your requests be made known to God.

Philippians 4:6 HCSB

Therefore don't worry about tomorrow, because tomorrow will worry about itself. Each day has enough trouble of its own.

Matthew 6:34 HCSB

Yea, though I walk through the valley of the shadow of death, I will fear no evil: for thou art with me; thy rod and thy staff they comfort me.

Psalm 23:4 KJV

I will be with you when you pass through the waters . . . when you walk through the fire . . . the flame will not burn you. For I the Lord your God, the Holy One of Israel, and your Savior.

Isaiah 43:2-3 HCSB

More Great Ideas

This life of faith, then, consists in just this—being a child in the Father's house. Let the ways of childish confidence and freedom from care, which so please you and win your heart when you observe your own little ones, teach you what you should be in your attitude toward God.

Hannah Whitall Smith

Today is mine. Tomorrow is none of my business. If I peer anxiously into the fog of the future, I will strain my spiritual eyes so that I will not see clearly what is required of me now.

Elisabeth Elliott

We are not called to be burden-bearers, but cross-bearers and light-bearers. We must cast our burdens on the Lord.

Corrie ten Boom

Worship and worry cannot live
in the same heart;
they are mutually exclusive.

—

Ruth Bell Graham

Today's Timely Tip

An important part of becoming a more mature Christian is learning to worry less and to trust God more.

Today's Prayer

Dear Lord, wherever I find myself, let me celebrate more and worry less. When my faith begins to waver, help me to trust You more. Then, with praise on my lips and the love of Your Son in my heart, let me live courageously, faithfully, prayerfully, and thankfully this day and every day. Amen

YOUR SHEPHERD

The Lord is my shepherd; I shall not want.

—

Psalm 23:1 KJV

Because we are imperfect human beings living imperfect lives, we worry. Even though we, as Christians, have the assurance of salvation—even though we, as believers, have the promise of God's love and protection—we find ourselves fretting over the countless details of everyday life. Jesus understood our concerns, and He addressed them.

In the 6th chapter of Matthew, Jesus makes it clear that the heart of God is a protective, caring heart:

Therefore I say to you, do not worry about your life, what you will eat or what you will drink; nor about your body, what you will put on. Is not life more than food and the body more than clothing? Look at the birds of the air, for they neither sow nor reap nor gather into barns; yet your Heavenly Father feeds them. Are you not of more value than they? Which of you by worrying can add one cubit to his stature? . . . Therefore do not worry about tomorrow, for tomorrow will worry about its own things. Sufficient for the day is its own trouble. (vv. 25-27, 34)

Perhaps you are uncertain about your future, your finances, your relationships, or your health. Or perhaps you are simply a "worrier" by nature. If so, make Matthew 6 a regular part of your daily Bible reading. This beautiful passage will remind you that God still sits in His heaven and you are His beloved child. Then, perhaps, you will worry a little less and trust God a little more, and that's as it should be because God is trustworthy . . . and you are protected.

Wisdom from God's Holy Word

Finally, my brethren, be strong in the Lord and in the power of His might. Put on the whole armor of God, that you may be able to stand against the wiles of the devil.

Ephesians 6:10-11 NKJV

The Lord your God in your midst, The Mighty One, will save; He will rejoice over you with gladness, He will quiet you with His love, He will rejoice over you with singing.

Zephaniah 3:17 NKJV

More Great Ideas

Our future may look fearfully intimidating, yet we can look up to the Engineer of the Universe, confident that nothing escapes His attention or slips out of the control of those strong hands.

Elisabeth Elliot

Only believe, don't fear. Our Master, Jesus, always watches over us, and no matter what the persecution, Jesus will surely overcome it.

Lottie Moon

God will never let you sink under your circumstances. He always provide a safety net and His love always encircles.

Barbara Johnson

A God wise enough to create me and the world I live in is wise enough to watch out for me.

Philip Yancey

Trials are not enemies of faith
but opportunities to reveal
God's faithfulness.

—

Barbara Johnson

Today's Timely Tip

You are protected by God . . . now and always.
The only security that lasts is the security that
flows from the loving heart of God.

Today's Prayer

Lord, You have promised to protect me, and I
will trust You. Today, I will live courageously
as I place my hopes, my faith, and life in Your
hands. Let my life be a testimony to the trans-
forming power of Your love, Your grace, and
Your Son. Amen

DAY 29

ENTHUSIASM
FOR THE JOURNEY

*Whatever you do, do it enthusiastically,
as something done for the Lord
and not for men.*

—

Colossians 3:23 HCSB

Can you truthfully say that you are an enthusiastic person? Are you passionate about your faith, your life, your family, and your future? Hopefully so. But if your zest for life has waned, it is now time to redirect your efforts and recharge your spiritual batteries. And that means refocusing your priorities by putting God first.

Each day is a glorious opportunity to serve God and to do His will. Are you enthused about life, or do you struggle through each day giving scarcely a thought to God's blessings? Are you constantly praising God for His gifts, and are you sharing His Good News with the world? And are you excited about the possibilities for service that God has placed before you, whether at home, at work, or at church? You should be.

Nothing is more important than your wholehearted commitment to God. Your faith must never be an afterthought; it must be your ultimate priority, your ultimate possession, and your ultimate passion. When you become passionate about your faith, you'll become passionate about your life, too.

Norman Vincent Peale advised, "Get absolutely enthralled with something. Throw yourself into it with abandon. Get out of yourself. Be somebody. Do something." His words apply to you. So don't settle for a lukewarm existence. Instead, make the character-building choice to become genuinely involved in life. The world needs your enthusiasm . . . and so do you.

Wisdom from God's Holy Word

I have seen that there is nothing better than for a person to enjoy his activities, because that is his reward. For who can enable him to see what will happen after he dies?

Ecclesiastes 3:22 HCSB

Do not lack diligence; be fervent in spirit; serve the Lord.

Romans 12:11 HCSB

He did it with all his heart. So he prospered.

2 Chronicles 31:21 NKJV

More Great Ideas

Your light is the truth of the Gospel message itself as well as your witness as to Who Jesus is and what He has done for you. Don't hide it.

Anne Graham Lotz

Making up a string of excuses is usually harder than doing the work.

Marie T. Freeman

Living life with a consistent spiritual walk deeply influences those we love most.

Vonette Bright

God is the giver, and we are the receivers. And His richest gifts are bestowed not upon those who do the greatest things, but upon those who accept His abundance and His grace.

Hannah Whitall Smith

Enthusiasm, like the flu, is contagious—we get it from one another.

Barbara Johnson

We act as though comfort
and luxury were the chief
requirements of life,
when all we need to make us
really happy is something
to be enthusiastic about.

—

Charles Kingsley

Today's Timely Tip

Don't wait for enthusiam to find you . . . go looking for it. Look at your life and your relationships as exciting adventures. Don't wait for life to spice itself; spice things up yourself.

Today's Prayer

Dear Lord, I know that others are watching the way that I live my life. Help me to be an enthusiastic Christian with a faith that is contagious. Amen

THE GIFT OF ETERNAL LIFE

And this is the testimony: God has given us
eternal life, and this life is in His Son.
The one who has the Son has life.
The one who doesn't have
the Son of God does not have life.

—

1 John 5:11-12 HCSB

Your life here on earth is merely a preparation for a far different life to come: the eternal life that God promises to those who welcome His Son into their hearts.

As a mere mortal, your vision for the future is finite. God's vision is not burdened by such limitations: His plans extend throughout all eternity. Thus, God's plans for you are not limited to the ups and downs of everyday life. Your Heavenly Father has bigger things in mind . . . much bigger things.

How marvelous it is that God became a man and walked among us. Had He not chosen to do so, we might feel removed from a distant Creator. But ours is not a distant God. Ours is a God who understands—far better than we ever could—the essence of what it means to be human.

God understands our hopes, our fears, and our temptations. He understands what it means to be angry and what it costs to forgive. He knows the heart, the conscience, and the soul of every person who has ever lived, including you.

As you struggle with the inevitable hardships and occasional disappointments of life, remember that God has invited you to accept His abundance not only for today but also for all eternity. So keep things in perspective. Although you will inevitably encounter occasional defeats in this world, you'll have all eternity to celebrate the ultimate victory in the next.

Wisdom from God's Holy Word

I have written these things to you who believe in the name of the Son of God, so that you may know that you have eternal life.

1 John 5:13 HCSB

Jesus said to her, "I am the resurrection and the life. The one who believes in Me, even if he dies, will live. Everyone who lives and believes in Me will never die—ever. Do you believe this?"

John 11:25-26 HCSB

More Great Ideas

If you are a believer, your judgment will not determine your eternal destiny. Christ's finished work on Calvary was applied to you the moment you accepted Christ as Savior.

Beth Moore

I can still hardly believe it. I, with shriveled, bent fingers, atrophied muscles, gnarled knees, and no feeling from the shoulders down, will one day have a new body—light, bright and clothed in righteousness—powerful and dazzling.

Joni Eareckson Tada

Your choice to either receive or reject the Lord Jesus Christ will determine where you spend eternity.

Anne Graham Lotz

The unfolding of our friendship with the Father will be a never-ending revelation stretching on into eternity.

Catherine Marshall

I now know the power of
the risen Lord! He lives!
The dawn of Easter
has broken in my own soul!
My night is gone!

—

Mrs. Charles E. Cowman

Today's Timely Tip

People love talking about religion, and everybody has their own opinions, but ultimately only one opinion counts . . . God's. Think about God's promise of eternal life—and what that promise means to you.

Today's Prayer

I know, Lord, that this world is not my home; I am only here for a brief while. And, You have given me the priceless gift of eternal life through Your Son Jesus. Keep the hope of heaven fresh in my heart, and, while I am in this world, help me to pass through it with faith in my heart and praise on my lips . . . for You. Amen

MORE FROM
GOD'S WORD
ABOUT . . .

Anger

A patient person [shows] great understanding, but a quick-tempered one promotes foolishness.

Proverbs 14:29 HCSB

But now you must also put away all the following: anger, wrath, malice, slander, and filthy language from your mouth.

Colossians 3:8 HCSB

All bitterness, anger and wrath, insult and slander must be removed from you, along with all wickedness. And be kind and compassionate to one another, forgiving one another, just as God also forgave you in Christ.

Ephesians 4:31-32 HCSB

Everyone must be quick to hear, slow to speak, and slow to anger, for man's anger does not accomplish God's righteousness.

James 1:19-20 HCSB

*Don't let your spirit rush
to be angry, for anger abides
in the heart of fools.*

—

Ecclesiastes 7:9 HCSB

Attitude

For the word of God is living and effective and sharper than any two-edged sword, penetrating as far as to divide soul, spirit, joints, and marrow; it is a judge of the ideas and thoughts of the heart.

Hebrews 4:12 HCSB

Make your own attitude that of Christ Jesus.

Philippians 2:5 HCSB

Set your minds on what is above, not on what is on the earth.

Colossians 3:2 HCSB

Finally brothers, whatever is true, whatever is honorable, whatever is just, whatever is pure, whatever is lovely, whatever is commendable—if there is any moral excellence and if there is any praise—dwell on these things.

Philippians 4:8 HCSB

Cheerfulness

A merry heart does good, like medicine.

Proverbs 17:22 NKJV

Is anyone cheerful? He should sing praises.

James 5:13 HCSB

A cheerful heart has a continual feast.

Proverbs 15:15 HCSB

Bright eyes cheer the heart; good news strengthens the bones.

Proverbs 15:30 HCSB

A joyful heart makes a face cheerful.

Proverbs 15:13 HCSB

Faith

If you do not stand firm in your faith, then you will not stand at all.

Isaiah 7:9 HCSB

Be alert, stand firm in the faith, be brave and strong.

1 Corinthians 16:13 HCSB

Now faith is the reality of what is hoped for, the proof of what is not seen.

Hebrews 11:1 HCSB

For we walk by faith, not by sight.

2 Corinthians 5:7 HCSB

Now without faith it is impossible to please God, for the one who draws near to Him must believe that He exists and rewards those who seek Him.

Hebrews 11:6 HCSB

Family

Choose for yourselves today the one you will worship . . . . As for me and my family, we will worship the Lord.

Joshua 24:15 HCSB

Now if anyone does not provide for his own relatives, and especially for his household, he has denied the faith and is worse than an unbeliever.

1 Timothy 5:8 HCSB

If a kingdom is divided against itself, that kingdom cannot stand. If a house is divided against itself, that house cannot stand.

Mark 3:24-25 HCSB

Love must be without hypocrisy. Detest evil; cling to what is good. Show family affection to one another with brotherly love. Outdo one another in showing honor.

Romans 12:9–10 HCSB

Loving God

He said to him, "You shall love the Lord your God with all your heart, with all your soul, and with all your mind. This is the greatest and most important commandment."

Matthew 22:37-38 HCSB

And we have this command from Him: the one who loves God must also love his brother.

1 John 4:21 HCSB

Love the Lord your God with all your heart, with all your soul, and with all your strength. These words that I am giving you today are to be in your heart. Repeat them to your children. Talk about them when you sit in your house and when you walk along the road, when you lie down and when you get up.

Deuteronomy 6:5-7 HCSB

For this is the love of God, that we keep His commandments. And His commandments are not burdensome.

1 John 5:3 NKJV

*We love Him
because He first loved us.*

—

1 John 4:19 NKJV

Materialism

And He told them, "Watch out and be on guard against all greed, because one's life is not in the abundance of his possessions."

Luke 12:15 HCSB

For what does it benefit a man to gain the whole world yet lose his life? What can a man give in exchange for his life?

Mark 8:36-37 HCSB

Don't collect for yourselves treasures on earth, where moth and rust destroy and where thieves break in and steal. But collect for yourselves treasures in heaven, where neither moth nor rust destroys, and where thieves don't break in and steal. For where your treasure is, there your heart will be also.

Matthew 6:19-21 HCSB

For the mind-set of the flesh is death, but the mind-set of the Spirit is life and peace.

Romans 8:6 HCSB

*Anyone trusting
in his riches will fall,
but the righteous
will flourish like foliage.*

—

Proverbs 11:28 HCSB

Temptation

No temptation has overtaken you except what is common to humanity. God is faithful and He will not allow you to be tempted beyond what you are able, but with the temptation He will also provide a way of escape, so that you are able to bear it.

1 Corinthians 10:13 HCSB

For we do not have a High Priest who cannot sympathize with our weaknesses, but was in all points tempted as we are, yet without sin. Let us therefore come boldly to the throne of grace, that we may obtain mercy and find grace to help in time of need.

Hebrews 4:15-16 NKJV

Be sober! Be on the alert! Your adversary the Devil is prowling around like a roaring lion, looking for anyone he can devour.

1 Peter 5:8 HCSB

The Lord knows how to deliver the godly out of temptations.

2 Peter 2:9 NKJV

*Put on the whole armor of God,
that you may be able to stand
against the wiles of the devil.*

—

Ephesians 6:11 NKJV

Testimony

But sanctify the Lord God in your hearts, and always be ready to give a defense to everyone who asks you a reason for the hope that is in you.

1 Peter 3:15 HCSB

You are the light of the world. A city that is set on a hill cannot be hidden. Nor do they light a lamp and put it under a basket, but on a lampstand, and it gives light to all who are in the house. Let your light so shine before men, that they may see your good works and glorify your Father in heaven.

Matthew 5:14–16 NKJV

Whatever I tell you in the dark, speak in the light; and what you hear in the ear, preach on the housetops.

Matthew 10:27 NKJV

But as for me, I will never boast about anything except the cross of our Lord Jesus Christ, through whom the world has been crucified to me, and I to the world.

Galatians 6:14 HCSB

*And I say to you,
anyone who acknowledges Me
before men, the Son of Man
will also acknowledge him before
the angels of God; but whoever
denies Me before men will be
denied before the angels of God.*

—

Luke 12:8-9 HCSB

Thanksgiving

Thanks be to God for His indescribable gift.

2 Corinthians 9:15 HCSB

And let the peace of the Messiah, to which you were also called in one body, control your hearts. Be thankful.

Colossians 3:15 HCSB

It is good to give thanks to the Lord, and to sing praises to Your name, O Most High.

Psalm 92:1 NKJV

Therefore as you have received Christ Jesus the Lord, walk in Him, rooted and built up in Him and established in the faith, just as you were taught, and overflowing with thankfulness.

Colossians 2:6-7 HCSB

Enter into His gates with thanksgiving, and into His courts with praise. Be thankful to Him, and bless His name. For the Lord is good; His mercy is everlasting, and His truth endures to all generations.

Psalm 100:4-5 NKJV

Wisdom

*The fear of the Lord is the beginning of wisdom;
a good understanding have all those who do His
commandments. His praise endures forever.*

Psalm 111:10 NKJV

*So teach us to number our days, that we may gain
a heart of wisdom.*

Psalm 90:12 NKJV

*A wise man will hear and increase learning, and
a man of understanding will attain wise counsel.*

Proverbs 1:5 NKJV

*Teach me, O Lord, the way of Your statutes, and
I shall keep it to the end.*

Psalm 119:33 NKJV

*Acquire wisdom—how much better it is than
gold! And acquire understanding—it is preferable
to silver.*

Proverbs 16:16 HCSB